REDISCOVERING *Me*

REDISCOVERING *You*

Couples Workbook

What No One Ever Told You About Relationships

includes quizzes, assessments, key insights,
proven strategies, and an individualized relationship profile

Michelle Jackson-McCoy, PhD

Rediscovering Me, Rediscovering You
Copyright © 2022 by Dr. Michelle Jackson-McCoy

ISBN 978-0-9727949-7-8
Requests for information should be directed to:
contact@bemontent.com

Printed in the United States.

You may also want to try…

What No One Ever Told Me About Me

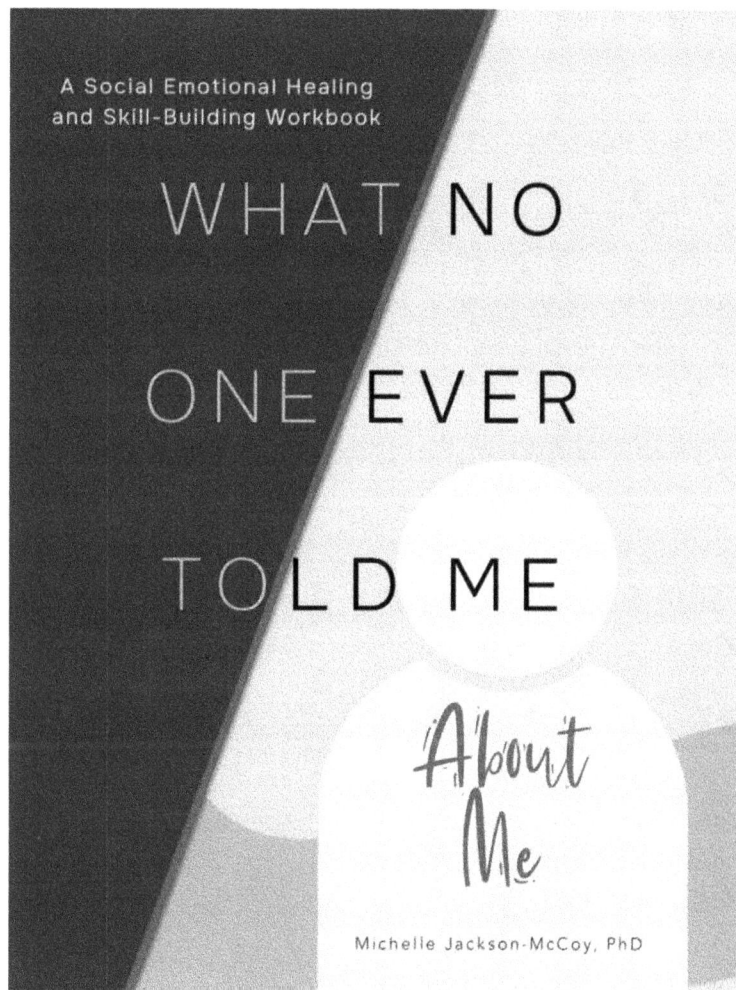

A guide for healing emotional wounds and learning the skills for staying healthy and whole! This penetrating resource delivers insights and strategies that are customized to your needs, your desires—your life.

REDISCOVERING *Me*

REDISCOVERING *You*

AT-A-GLANCE

GETTING STARTED

About 2

Features 2

TOPICS

ABOUT

Rediscovering Me, Rediscovering You is a comprehensive workbook for couples. Whether your goal is relationship enhancement, restoration, reconciliation, or to have fun, this workbook is designed for you! *Rediscovering Me Rediscovering You* delivers insight, personal discoveries, and a unique lens from which to experience the clearest view you've ever had of your relationship.

FEATURES

Clinically-based	Clinical insights serve as the foundation for early identification and intervention with issues that traditionally challenge relationships and the ability to achieve oneness.
Activity-driven	*Rediscovering Me Rediscovering You* is based on the concept that experiences are easier to remember than information. Experiences are augmented by information and revelations which are documented in the couples' workbooks. Ultimately, each workbook becomes a reference and a keepsake.
Privacy-protected	A core component of the workbook is "privacy." The only individual that will see any workbook responses is your partner. Privacy and confidentiality are premium.
Adventurous	Couples will experience new insights as they explore relevant topics and reexamine old topics using a completely fresh lens. The goal is to enjoy an in-depth journey into everything no one ever told you about relationships
Life-changing	*Rediscovering Me Rediscovering You* doesn't just offer valuable relationship and life tools, *Rediscovering Me Rediscovering You* helps create an atmosphere where transformations begin!
User-friendly	No lengthy preparation needed. Just open the workbooks and you're ready to begin! All the instructions, worksheets, assessments, and commentary are in one book to ensure easy implementation.
Enjoyable	Using a combination of humor, surprise, wit and opportunities for self-exploration and life-changing revelations each element is designed to be meaningful, memorable, and for couples to enjoy the adventure of discovering.

This workbook includes the Discovery Inventory, ten different relationship scales, an individualized relationship profile, and numerous time-proven insights and strategies for an immersive, life-changing journey. All the tools needed are packaged in this one workbook for your convenience.

YOUR JOURNEY BEGINS!

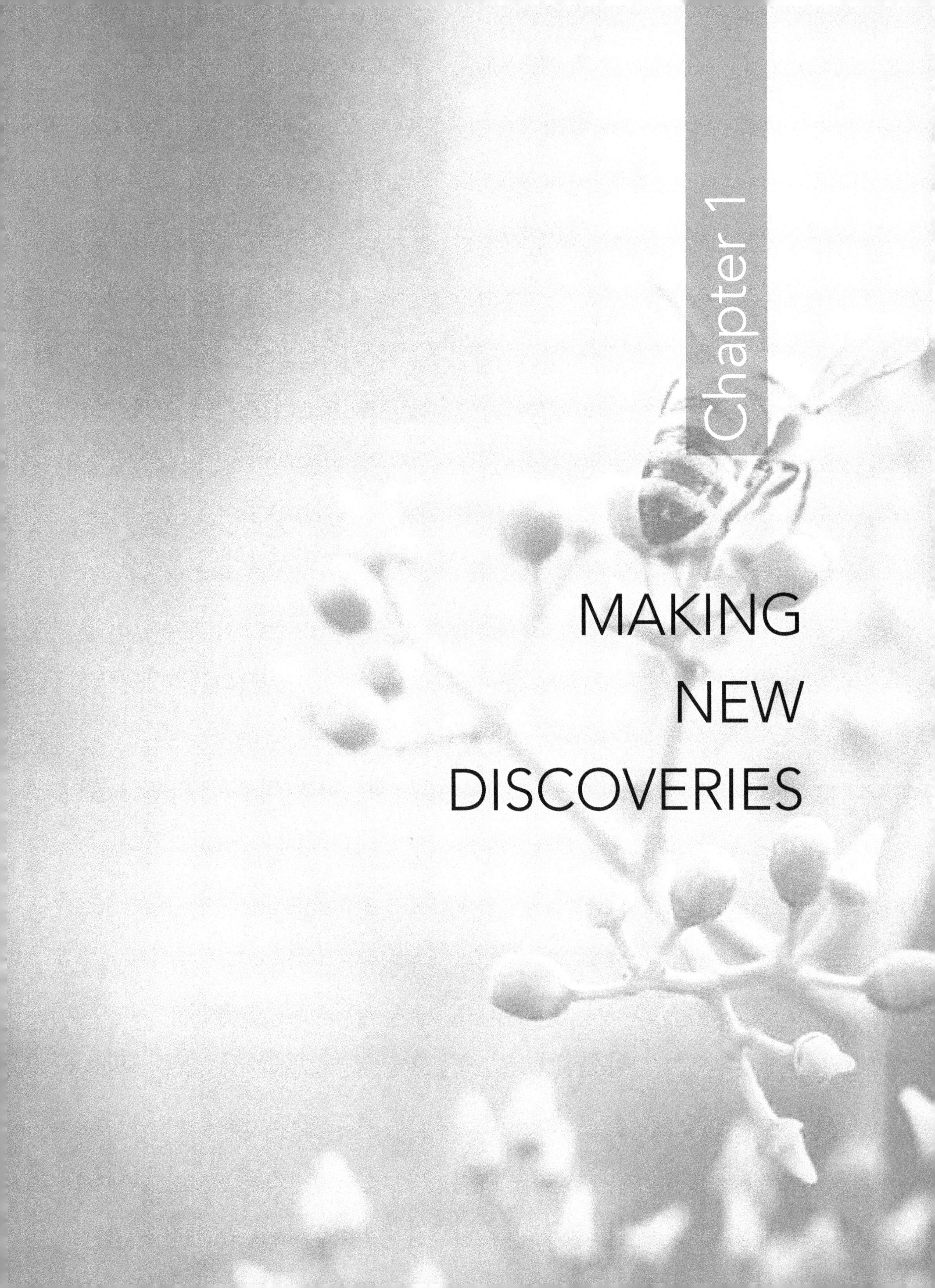

Chapter 1

MAKING NEW DISCOVERIES

JOURNEY NOTES

It is so amazing that you can enter a relationship with a person and several years later still make discoveries and gain new insights into their life. As you will see, this workbook embraces the experience of discovery and rediscovery. To jumpstart the process, we have developed a "Discovery Inventory." Take a moment to complete this valuable tool. Only your partner will see your responses to the questions, and there are no right or wrong answers. Consider the inventory your chance to very honestly and lovingly share with your partner information that will place your relationship on an even higher road to happiness. Take this opportunity to arm your partner and yourself with information to meet your relationship needs. One clue about discoveries is that your findings will be no greater than your willingness to embrace the adventure. If you fear the adventure, your discoveries will go no farther than what you already know. The depth of your discovery is up to you. We hope you enjoy this exciting journey as you enter the world of *Rediscovering Me Rediscovering You.*

My Discovery Inventory

Here are questions many couples never think to ask each other until years later in their relationship. They either spend years guessing what the answers might be, or they spend years not realizing this is information they need to know.

INSTRUCTIONS: Take a few minutes to complete the ten questions in the Discovery Inventory. Please do not consult with your partner and be as truthful as possible.

1. What are your three greatest unmet needs?

    1. _____

       _____

    2. _____

       _____

    3. _____

       _____

INSIGHT 1
Unmet needs are actually unfulfilled expectations.

2. What three qualities do you most appreciate about your partner?

    1. _____

       _____

    2. _____

       _____

    3. _____

       _____

INSIGHT 2
These are ways your needs are met through the natural qualities your partner brings to the relationship.

3. I am happiest in our relationship when my partner:

INSIGHT 3

These are behaviors
your partner may want
to consider turning
into habits.

4. I express love to my mate in the following ways:

INSIGHT 4

It is important to ask
yourself, "Am I
expressing love in a
manner that my
partner can recognize
and in a style he/she
desires?"

5. My partner irritates me most when:

INSIGHT 5

Here is where
communication problems
are born. Most couples
either: Say nothing, wait
too long to say something,
or communicate in a
manner that makes it hard
for their partner to hear.

6. I hurt most in our relationship when my partner:

INSIGHT 6

This is where your
partner needs to
examine their response
to your pain and answer
the question, "What
would love do?"

7.   What is it about you that your partner is trying to
     change, and you wish they would accept?

INSIGHT 7

These are areas where
a wise, caring, and
impartial outsider may
help each of you see
yourselves more clearly.

8.   When you first met, what attracted you to
     your partner?

INSIGHT 8

These are things your
partner should hear
you say.

9.   What do you find most attractive about your
     partner today?

INSIGHT 9

These are things your
partner should hear
you say.

10. If you were speaking to your partner, how would
     you complete this statement: "I wish you better
     understood this about me."

INSIGHT 10

These are areas where
you may not have
communicated clearly. Or
your partner may not
desire to understand and
hear when you
communicate about these
areas of your life.

In relationships, so much of what challenges us is not about each other's faults; it's about each
other's unmet needs. Part of what you did in this inventory was to discover one another's needs.

NOTES

_____

_____

_____

_____

_____

_____

_____

_____

_____

_____

_____

_____

_____

_____

_____

_____

_____

_____

_____

NOTES

NOTES

_____

_____

_____

_____

_____

_____

_____

_____

_____

_____

_____

_____

_____

_____

_____

_____

_____

_____

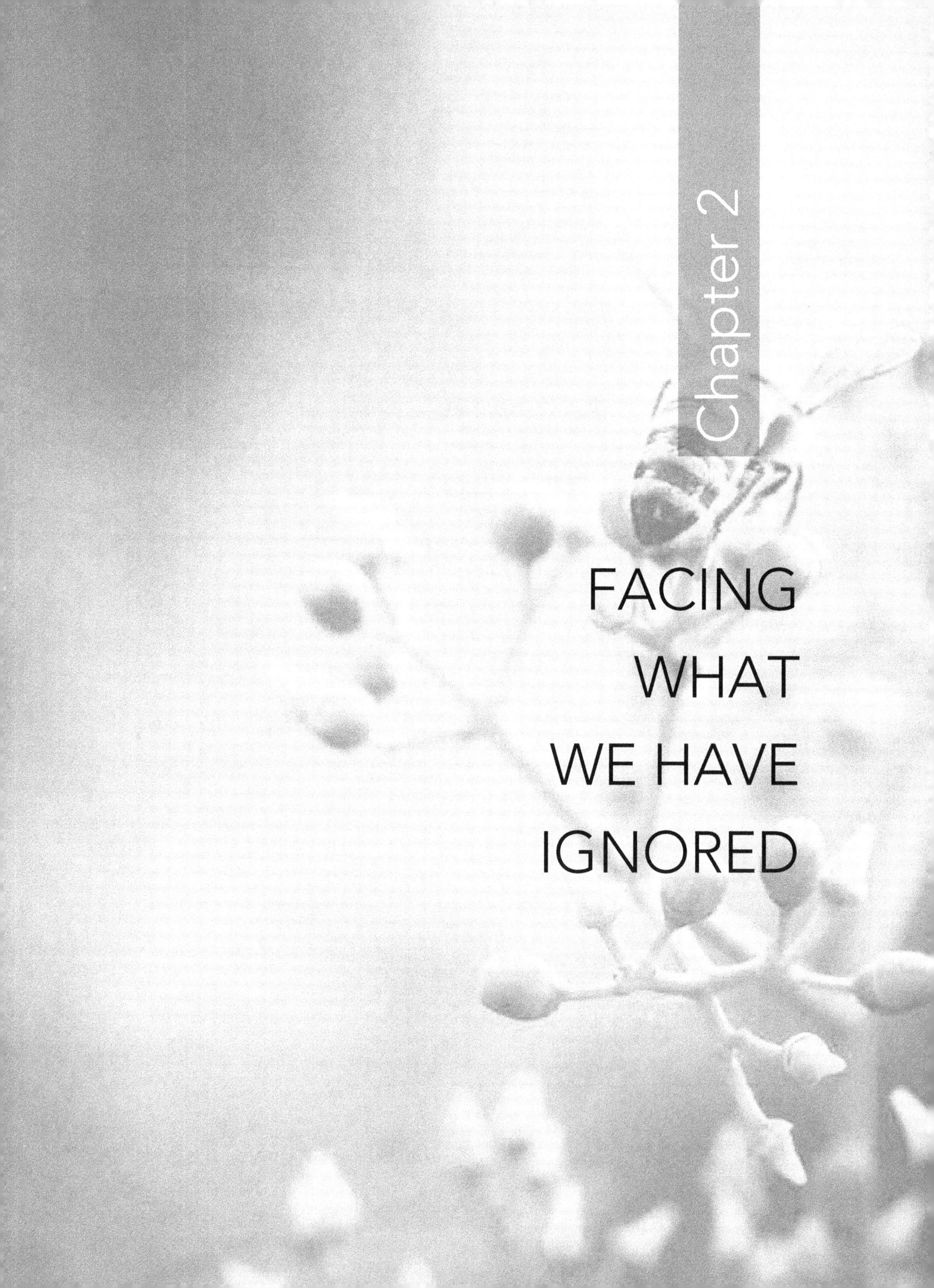

Chapter 2

FACING WHAT WE HAVE IGNORED

JOURNEY NOTES

In the movies, you meet the person of your dreams, fall in love, and live happily ever after. In reality, the road to happily ever after has a few more twists and turns. The twists and turns come from the needs, wants, voids, fears, and past experiences we bring to our relationships. In other words, while your partner is attracted to all the ways you are amazing, they must also prepare themselves to eventually face all the ways in which you think you are not. What do we do with what we may consider the least attractive parts of ourselves? Typically, we try to keep them hidden and under control. What you will discover in this chapter is that so much of what is suppressing your ability to achieve the relationship you are hoping for is your belief that some issues will eventually go away with time. Are we talking about every issue in your life? No, humans come with issues. We can't change that fact. We are only discussing issues preventing you from discovering the life and relationships you desire. If there are issues that have become reoccurring themes in your life and consistently reappear in your relationships, it is safe to say those won't go away with time. They go away with attention.

Let's Reminisce!

Whether you are seriously dating, married, or just considering it, think back to when the two of you decided to commit to one another. What was your **#1** reason for wanting to commit?

INSTRUCTIONS: Below is a list of unhealthy reasons to commit. These reasons will not apply to everyone. As you complete the checklist, keep in mind that we are asking you to identify reasons that may have, in big or small ways, influenced your decision to commit or consider committing to your partner and your partner's reasons for wanting to commit to you.

Scale 1 Unhealthy Reasons to Commit (Place an "X" next to the reasons that relate to either you or your partner)	It is at least a small part of **my** reason	It is at least a small part of my **partner's** reason	Insights to Consider
Escape – Attempting to free yourself from an unpleasant or confining situation (e.g., strict parents, a controlling ex-wife/ex-husband).			An indication of how you deal with conflict. Be careful not to bring this style of problem-solving to your relationship.
Time/Age – Pressure from you or others that you are at risk of overstaying your status as a bachelor/bachelorette or that your biological clock is ticking.			Don't let your biological clock cheat you out of the relationship you desire and deserve. Those clocks tick loudly and often scare away the person that is genuinely looking for love.
Prestige – A desire for status or social recognition.			You don't find your worth in a relationship. You bring it to your relationship.
Poor Self-Concept – Searching for a more meaningful life while finding it difficult to appreciate your self-worth.			These are the symptoms of a battered spirit and can be challenging to heal.
Rebound – Attempting to eliminate the feeling of rejection, disappointment, or loneliness due to a previous relationship by immediately finding and entering a new relationship.			This means you are creating new expectations for a new relationship without time to develop a clear and healthy outlook on your past relationships.
Pregnancy – Fear of shame and condemnation and/or a desire to make the situation "right."			The relationship must now work to catch up to your experiences.
Sexual Attraction – Strong sexual desires became a driving force for critical decisions regarding your future.			Be careful making life altering decisions based upon urges. It can cause you to overlook the more important work needed to sustain a healthy, happy relationship.
Guilt/Obligation – Choosing to be "responsible" in your decision-making to avoid remorse, regret, or shame.			Guilty decisions often lead to regret (what you feel), which can lead to resentment (what you manifest as you grieve your past).
Financial Gain – Attempting to ease your financial burden.			It is important to remember that your relationship is not a business.

If you placed an "X" on any of the reasons listed in Scale 1:

Ask yourself | Has this been fully resolved, or does it remain as a factor that, in big or small ways, is impacting our relationship? *(Place an "X" in one of the boxes below next to the answer you view as most accurate.)*

☐ The issue(s) are fully resolved.

☐ The issue(s) are <u>not</u> fully resolved.

Is committing for unhealthy reasons a death sentence for a relationship?

No, it is not a death sentence for a relationship.

It simply means there are issues you and your partner must address to reach the fullness you want to experience in your relationship.

Now you are beginning to address "foundational issues." These are thoughts, beliefs, and behaviors you and your partner acquired before your commitment that often create challenges in developing a strong foundation to sustain a fulfilling relationship.

Just A Thought | Remember, some things heal with time but most things heal with attention. The third option is to lower the standard for what you define as a "good" relationship. What choice have you made?

Let's talk about solutions

Notice that most unhealthy reasons to commit involve reasoning that causes you to view your partner as a solution to a problem or concern. This does **not** imply you don't care deeply for your partner. However, it does indicate you also were using reasoning to solve what you viewed as a concerning "problem" or "issue" in your life.

One of the most powerful forces in relationships

There is a force more powerful than reasoning. It is one of the most powerful forces that can enter and elevate your relationship. What is it? It is—passion.

What is passion? | Passion is a state of affection that operates more from emotion than reasoning.

Relationships are "fueled" by passion, but that does not mean you always "feel" passion. It is an underlying force driving your behavior and results in a more positive and elevated relationship experience.

What attitudes, beliefs, or behaviors are functioning as barriers to increasing the passion in your relationship? *(Write your answer below.)*

As you think about your response to the question above, remember…

A Few Things to Remember

1. Your lack of passion or lack of expressed passion is not due to your personality type. No personality type can overpower the heart if you decide to move past your fears.

2. A lack of passion in your relationship usually is not caused by a lack of love or a lack of sex. It typically indicates there is a lack of intimacy.

3. It is not anyone else's responsibility to uplift your partner. The journey to a more fulfilling relationship requires your participation.

4. Don't leave voids in your relationship. There is a law of physics that whenever a void exists, something rushes to fill it. The same is true in relationships. If you are unwilling to meet your partner's needs, you are leaving the relationship vulnerable to those outside of your relationship who may have an interest in meeting your partner's needs.

5. Your relationship may survive without passion, but it will never reach its full potential until you include it.

6. When asked, "Why don't you uplift your partner or show passion in your relationship?" Saying "I don't know" is a dishonest answer to a very important question. You may not care enough to talk about it; you may not have the courage to say what you are thinking, or you may choose to pretend the issue doesn't exist. But for sure, you have the answer.

7. Not only do we enjoy being the recipient of passion, but our human nature desires and requires it.

How to increase passion

What is the key to unleashing passion in your relationship?

The key to passion is intimacy.

The journey to intimacy can be a hard road to travel because it is not as focused on your behavior as it is focused on your heart. But there are a few strategies you can use to stir those feelings.

Tips to Move You Down the Pathway Towards Intimacy

1. Don't be afraid to state the obvious positive. In other words, if your partner is attractive, don't feel that because they are aware of their attractiveness there is no need for you to tell them. Sincere affirmations and statements of inspiration always feel good.

2. Remember, a clumsy affectionate sentence written or stated by you will always beat a well-stated store-bought card. This is not to suggest that you stop buying cards, but at some point, you must also speak for yourself.

3. Don't overestimate the shelf-life of a compliment. Your partner shouldn't have to think back too far to remember the last time you gave one.

4. Sex should be a celebration of oneness and an expression of passion. It should not become a bargaining chip in the relationship. Beware of allowing ulterior motives to define and control your bedroom.

5. Treat yourself in a way that is consistent with how you want to be perceived and treated by your partner.

6. Desire to be an inspiration to your partner. No matter how long you have been together, your partner never gets tired of seeing and being inspired by the best version of you.

For those who want to begin the process of rekindling the fire, what will you commit to doing this week to bring more passion into your relationship? *(Describe below.)*

Recommended Activity

Each couple should set aside time to share one another's discoveries from your workbooks. While sharing, it is important that you operate within the "Sharing Guidelines" outlined below. **Remember, at this point, all your questions should be asked of yourself, not your partner.**

Sharing Guidelines

Whatever your partner has written in their workbook represents what they feel, how they view it, and what they believe to be true.

For the remainder of this experience, we are asking you to eliminate two words from your vocabulary, the words "right" and "wrong." Apart from infidelity or abuse, there is seldom an instance of someone being "right" or "wrong" when discussing their relationship. You are usually addressing perceptions—how I see it and how you see it.

Once you move past the concepts of "right" and "wrong" you will see that your private sharing times are opportunities to ask questions of **YOURSELF.** Let the following three questions serve as a guide:

1. How do I feel about the way my partner views me and our relationship?

2. What is it about my attitude, beliefs, and/or behaviors that cause my partner to feel the way they do about me?

3. What can I do to improve my relationship with my partner?

Hmmm... | Why did we spend so much time identifying potential challenges to your relationship?

We spent that time because we want to be specific in identifying areas within your relationship that need healing and enrichment.

One of the most important gifts we hope you take from this workbook experience is not only identifying the mountains and valleys in your relationship, but also learning how to come together as a couple and take the fuel out of whatever may be challenging your relationship.

First, we must acknowledge that every challenge in your relationship is an opportunity to learn how to rise. The question you must now answer is, "What will you do with this opportunity?

NOTES

_____

_____

_____

_____

_____

_____

_____

_____

_____

_____

_____

_____

_____

_____

_____

_____

_____

_____

_____

NOTES

_____

_____

_____

_____

_____

_____

_____

_____

_____

_____

_____

_____

_____

_____

_____

_____

_____

_____

_____

NOTES

_____

_____

_____

_____

_____

_____

_____

_____

_____

_____

_____

_____

_____

_____

_____

_____

_____

_____

_____

_____

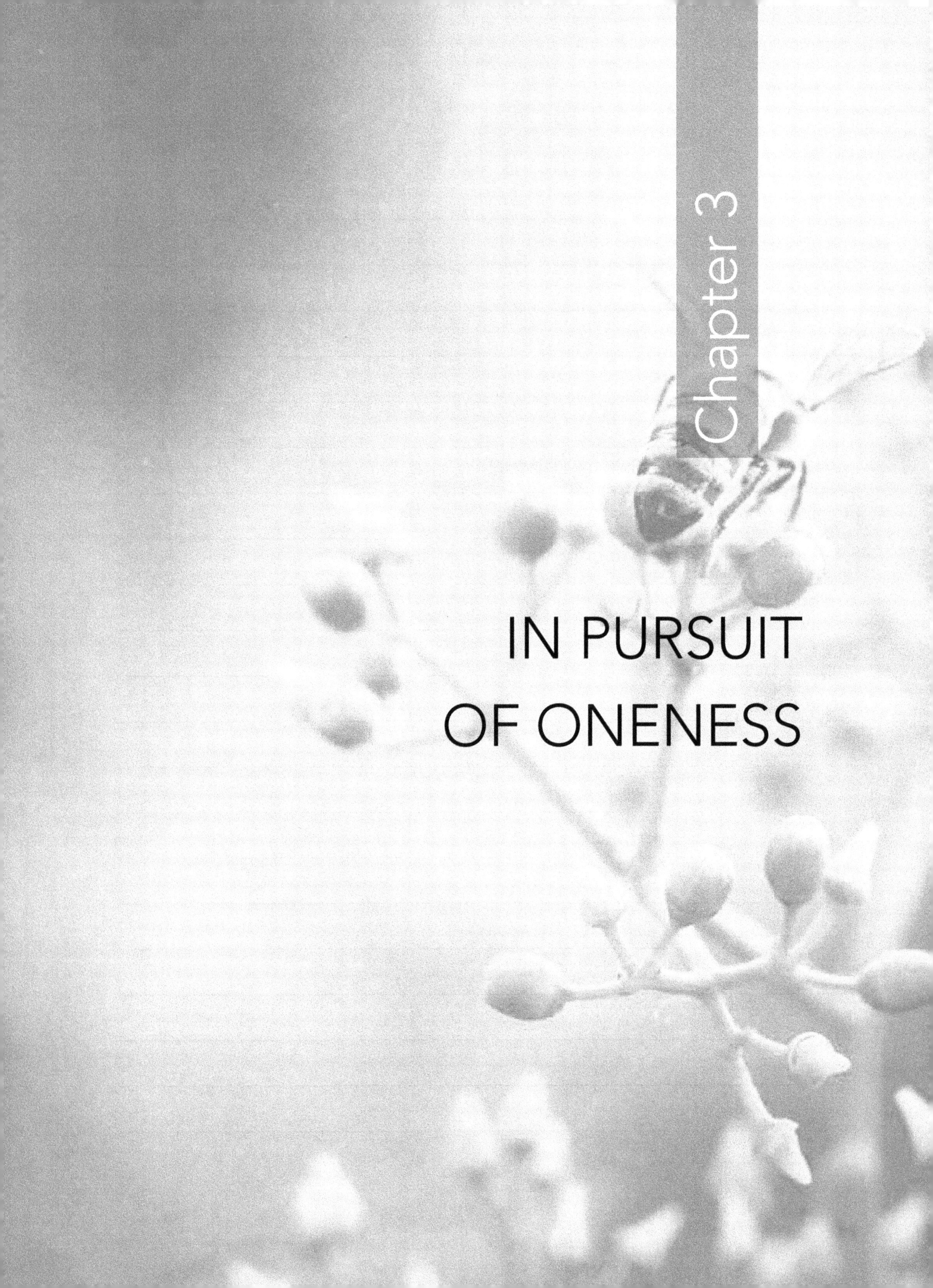

Chapter 3

IN PURSUIT OF ONENESS

JOURNEY NOTES

"Oneness." It is such a small term that has such a significant meaning. Amazingly, this little seven-letter word can present one of the greatest challenges in your relationship. But should you and your partner decide to make "oneness" a goal, the rewards are worth the pursuit. The three beautiful gifts oneness gives are harmony, unity, and a stronger foundation on which to build your relationship. In fact, it is impossible to experience the fullness of your relationship without it. Achieving oneness is the key that unlocks the essence of what love relationships are all about—connecting with someone in a manner that enables you to authentically express and experience your highest levels of fulfillment.

In Pursuit of Oneness

The definition of oneness	Oneness is the blending of separate lives and agendas to create one unified entity with a greater purpose than that which can be accomplished apart from one another.

Except during sex, describe the moments in your relationship when you are the most connected to your partner.

_____

Just A Thought	Just as there are situations that encourage oneness, there are situations that threaten oneness.

What are the threats to oneness?

INSTRUCTIONS: Make a list of things you view as potential threats to developing oneness between you and your partner. Try to be specific in your answer. For example, instead of writing "my job," be more specific by writing, "I work too many hours per day."

1. _____

2. _____

3. _____

4. _____

5. _____

6. _____

Three Types of Threats to Relationships

Threat #1 — **Individual Threats**
Threats that originate from your personality, temperament, and worldview.

Threat #2 — **Relationship Threats**
Threats that originate from the combination of you and your partner's personality, temperament, and background coming together.

Threat #3 — **External Threats**
Threats that exist outside of the relationship but can have a powerful impact on the relationship.

Looking at your relationship, can you think of examples for each type of threat?

INSTRUCTIONS: Using the table below, place the threats you wrote on page 24 into the correct columns below. This will provide you with a clearer view of the types of threats having the greatest impact on your relationship.

Individual Threats ("I" Statements)	Relationship Threats ("We" Statements)	External Threats ("They" Statements)
Example: I don't have patience with my partner.	**Example:** We (my partner and I) have different and conflicting religious beliefs.	**Example:** They (our in-laws) are overly involved in our relationship.

Common threats to oneness

INSTRUCTIONS: Place an "X" next to the threats that are most relevant to you and your partner. It is ok to have more than one "X" for a threat if it is a threat for both you and your partner.

Scale 2
Threats to Oneness
(Place an "X" on all that apply)

You	Your Partner	**Individual Threats** *(within yourself)*
___	___	Selfishness
___	___	Difficulty with commitment
___	___	Lack of self-control
___	___	Poor problem-solving skills
___	___	Controlling personality
___	___	Dishonesty
___	___	Difficulty being romantically expressive or receptive

Relationship Threats *(within your relationship)*

You	Your Partner	
___	___	Poor communication skills
___	___	A lack of quality time together
___	___	Differences in character, personality, and perspective
___	___	Different expectations regarding roles and responsibilities within the relationship
___	___	Differences in personal history (i.e., values, religion, politics, socioeconomic status)

External Threats *(outside of your relationship)*

You	Your Partner	
___	___	Allowing individuals outside of your relationship to be overly involved and influential in your relationship (i.e., in-laws, friends, etc.)
___	___	Extramarital affairs such as infidelity, career, hobby obsessions, materialism, apathy, or being overly occupied with family or friends

Just A Thought	If you want to discover the traits for having a healthy relationship, look at the opposite of the threat. For example, if the threat is "dishonesty" the healthy trait you may want to increase in your relationship is "honesty."

How to increase oneness

Now that you have identified some of the threats in your relationship let's talk about some safeguards that increase your experience of oneness.

Scale 3 Qualities That Increase Oneness *(Place an "X" next to qualities you or your partner DO NOT show enough of in your relationship.)*	Qualities I **DO NOT** show enough of in our relationship	Qualities my partner **DOES NOT** show enough of in our relationship
Love - Your readiness to sacrificially give to someone other than yourself.		
Joy - An authentic happiness.		
Peace - A serenity of your mind characterized by an absence of conflict behaviors and fear.		
Long-Suffering - Your patience with others and yourself as you demonstrate your ability to calmly endure life's challenges.		
Gentleness - Your display of kindness.		
Goodness - Your generosity.		
Faithfulness - Your loyalty and trustworthiness.		
Humility - Freedom from pride or arrogance while demonstrating consideration for others.		
Temperance - Your ability to demonstrate self-control despite your strongest desire to express anger or frustration.		

INSTRUCTIONS: Write the total number of "X's" for each column in the shaded areas below.

Total	Total Number (Me)	Total Number (My Partner)

Important Note

Expect to see "X's" in Scale 3. We all are a work in progress. The purpose of Scale 3 is to reveal where the work needs to occur in your relationship. As you look at the qualities that are missing in your relationship, don't forget to recognize and appreciate all that you are bringing to your relationship. Even the happiest couples still identify areas where they need to grow.

Just A Thought

These qualities make great goals for our lives. Just remember, these qualities count as being present in your life only when they are recognizable by someone other than you. If you're the only one that can see it, there is probably more work for you to do.

Recommended Activity

Develop a solution for each threat you have identified in Scale 2 on page 26. Solutions should be something you and your partner view as reasonable for both of you to implement.

NOTES

_____

_____

_____

_____

_____

_____

_____

_____

_____

_____

_____

_____

_____

_____

_____

_____

_____

_____

NOTES

_____

_____

_____

_____

_____

_____

_____

_____

_____

_____

_____

_____

_____

_____

_____

_____

_____

_____

_____

NOTES

_____

_____

_____

_____

_____

_____

_____

_____

_____

_____

_____

_____

_____

_____

_____

_____

_____

_____

_____

Chapter 4

IDENTIFYING AND
EXAMINING OUR
EXPECTATIONS

JOURNEY NOTES

You take them with you everywhere you go, and they work hard and swiftly defining all your relationships. What are they? They're "expectations." Which are perspectives created from our assumptions about the world and our role in it. Expectations answer the perpetual question we instinctively ask, "What do I anticipate?" They appear harmless but can be quite lethal in relationships—especially when what we expect from others doesn't match what they expect of themselves. Beware! The trick is to find the balance. Too few of them can leave us feeling disappointed and compromised, and too many can leave us lonely and alone.

Identifying and Examining
Our Expectations

Clarifying our expectations

INSTRUCTIONS: Use the space below to list expectations you have of your partner as it relates to your relationship. At this point, **only complete Column 1.** Leave Columns 2 through 5 blank for now. They will be completed later.

Column 1 Scale 4 My Relationship Expectations *(List 10 things you expect from your partner)*	Column 2 I satisfy this expectation in my relationship	Column 3 This should not be expected of me	Column 4 This expectation is difficult for me to satisfy	Column 5 This is an expectation I would like to achieve
1				
2				
3				
4				
5				
6				
7				
8				
9				
10				

Clarifying your partner's expectations

Use the space below to make a list of what you think are your partner's expectations of you. At this point, **only complete column 6**. Columns 7 and 8 will be completed later.

	Column 6	Column 7	Column 8
	Scale 5 My Partner's Relationship Expectations *(List 10 things you believe your partner expects from you within your relationship)*	Accurate	Inaccurate
1			
2			
3			
4			
5			
6			
7			
8			
9			
10			

INSTRUCTIONS: After you have completed Column 6, give your workbook to your partner. Your partner will then complete columns 2, 3, 4, 5, 7, and 8 in your workbook by placing an "X" in the columns as they deem appropriate. After your partner has completed their entries, they should return the workbook to you.

INSTRUCTIONS: After the workbooks have been returned, please examine where your partner has placed an "X" in each column. Circle the "X" if you disagree.

Just A Thought

This exercise can serve as a wonderful starting point to initiate healthy discussions regarding misconceptions and miscommunications.

Expectations are the lens through which the heart is revealed

What we desire is manifested through our expectations. Looking back at Scales 4 and 5, what do your expectations tell you about yourself and your partner? *(Write your answer below.)*

The power and importance of expectations

Expectations are the underlying force that determines where you "set the bar" in your relationship. When you continually are unable to please your partner, it is usually an indication of a difference in expectations.

The key is for you and your partner to have the courage to discuss each other's expectations. If you find the courage, you will discover a wonderful world of insights into your partner's dreams, desires, and wishes. Examining expectations will take you a long way toward oneness.

Not all expectations are good expectations

It would be unwise to talk about expectations and not discuss the most problematic type of expectations that plague so many couples. What are they? They are unrealistic expectations. These are expectations that set the bar too high, are impractical or idealistic, and typically result in disappointments that are near impossible for the couple to resolve. An unachievable standard dictating what you view as successes and failures in your relationship. Although they are poison to a relationship, the healthy couple is the one that expects unrealistic expectations to pop up in their relationship. What we are saying is that it is normal for them to appear. But it is detrimental to allow them to stay.

The expectations couples are afraid to talk about—mismatched expectations

Mismatched expectations occur when the expectations you have of yourself do not match the expectations your partner has of you. The reverse also happens when the expectations your partner has of themselves do not match the expectations you have of them.

Three Keys to Healing Mismatched Expectations

Examination
Find the courage to examine where you have set the bar in your relationship. It is important to remember that not all expectations are realistic. Unrealistic expectations need to be quickly addressed.

Communication
You may not think about it this way, but communication is a life skill. It is such an important topic, we dedicated an entire chapter to communication later in the workbook. Let's just say, your exaggerated body language and timely eye rolls are not sufficient to effectively communicate where you have set the bar in the

Understanding
Keep in mind that being understanding is only the key for expectations that yield respect, incorporate compassion, and retains your dignity. Expectations that require you to submit to any form of abuse, denies you of your dignity, or compromises your basic human rights should be met with a response that has your health and safety as a priority.

What about the unexpected?

The "unexpected" represent unanticipated events that happen to couples, often due to no intent or planning of their own (e.g., losing your job, suffering a medical injury, having a child that is physically challenged, or has other special needs). These occurrences can create the greatest challenges for your relationship.

Some of you never learned how to overcome difficulties and hard times. So, you do everything a powerless person would do. You blame, avoid, get angry, get even, and more. In these challenging moments, you must find your voice and recognize that you have the power of choice. You have the power to make other choices for your life and respond to life events in a manner that can change your course and put you on a more positive and productive trajectory.

Taking Action Steps

(SUPPLIES: A sheet of paper and pencil/pen)

Step #1   On a sheet of paper, write down what areas of your relationship you would like to heal. Be specific. Don't just say, "improve our relationship." Specifically identify your desires so you can directly address them.

Step #2   After you have completed your list, show it to your partner so the two of you can agree.

Step #3   Fold the paper and place it in the center of the room as you and your partner agree to turn a new page in your relationship, leave old mindsets in the past, and walk towards health and healing in those areas indicated on the paper.

Step #4   As a couple, walk away from the paper. This will symbolize that you agree to leave old unhealthy behaviors and expectations in the past. As you walk away, you are agreeing to work towards moving forward without those unfair and unhelpful behaviors and mindsets.

Recommended Activity

Set aside time this week to discuss your thoughts about the expectations discovered through your work in this chapter. Remember, all discussions should occur using the Sharing Guidelines, which are included below as a reminder.

Sharing Guidelines

Whatever your partner has written in their workbook represents what they feel, how they view it, and what they believe to be true.

For the remainder of this experience, we are asking you to eliminate two words from your vocabulary: "right" and "wrong." Apart from infidelity or abuse, there is seldom an instance of someone being "right" or "wrong" when discussing their relationship. You are usually addressing perceptions—how I see it and how you see it.

Once you move past the concepts of "right" and "wrong," you will see that your private sharing times are opportunities to ask questions of **YOURSELF**. Let the following three questions serve as a guide:

1. How do I feel about the way my partner views me and our relationship?

2. What is it about my attitude, beliefs, and/or behaviors that cause my partner to feel the way they do about me?

3. What can I do to improve my relationship with my partner?

NOTES

NOTES

NOTES

_____

_____

_____

_____

_____

_____

_____

_____

_____

_____

_____

_____

_____

_____

_____

_____

_____

_____

_____

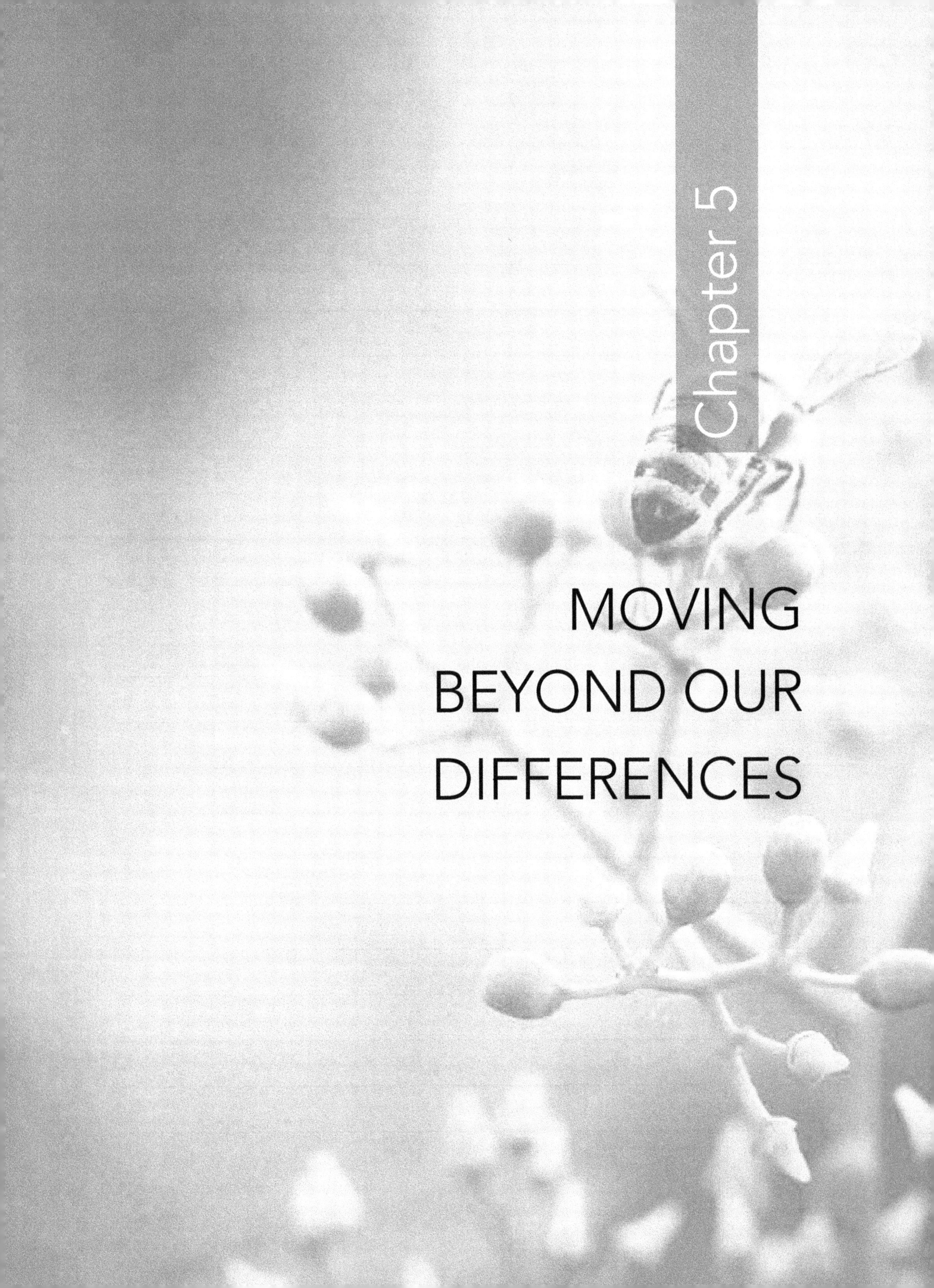

Chapter 5

MOVING BEYOND OUR DIFFERENCES

JOURNEY NOTES

Oftentimes, we enthusiastically choose to enter relationships because we find that special someone with whom we have so many things in common. But from the moment we enter the relationship, we begin discovering differences. Some of those differences we may view as a refreshing contrast to our personality. However, other differences can cause us to pause and say, "hmmm…" What seems most peculiar is that we are surprised every time we find a difference. Why are we surprised? We are surprised because differences are not usually part of our expectations for those we select as our partners. Herein is the challenge for every relationship. How do we move beyond the differences and rediscover what we enjoyed in the beginning? Well, we can't go back, but forward can be a great choice if armed with the right tools.

.

Moving Beyond Our Differences

As we move into Chapters 5 and 6, you will see that sometimes we are so busy evaluating whether our partner is meeting our expectations we don't realize how long ago we stopped meeting theirs.

In this chapter, we ask you to set aside your "What I Need You to Be for Me" list. This list is one of the biggest threats to relationships. Why? It is a threat because the list keeps you focused on "blame," which traps you in the past. Your focus on the past distracts you from reaching forward toward health and healing in your relationship. As we move through this chapter, you will see that our obsession with "blame" is a significant factor that cheats most couples out of a stronger and more satisfying relationship.

Similarities and differences

INSTRUCTIONS: Take a moment to answer the following three questions:

1. My partner and I are similar in the following ways:

2. My partner and I are different in the following ways:

3. Which of the abovementioned differences do you think presents a challenge to your relationship or could threaten your efforts to achieve/maintain oneness? *(Please explain.)*

Reacting to the Differences

What are your usual responses to the differences listed in Question #2 on the previous page? *(Check all that apply.)*

_____ You try to convince your partner to change

_____ You try to ignore the differences

_____ You withdraw from your partner

_____ You accept the differences without trying to change your partner

_____ You criticize your partner

_____ You argue

What responses does your partner usually have to the differences listed on the previous page? *(Check all that apply. Then share your responses with your partner. No need to exchange workbooks. Just showing your responses to your partner will be sufficient.)*

_____ Your partner tries to convince you to change

_____ Your partner tries to ignore the differences

_____ Your partner withdraws

_____ Your partner accepts the differences without trying to change you

_____ Your partner criticizes you

_____ Your partner argues

Based on what you saw in your partner's workbook, how do your partner's responses make you feel? *(Describe below.)*

INSTRUCTIONS: After you have finished writing, exchange workbooks and see where you and your partner agree and where you disagree.

What is a popular first response to differences within a relationship?

A typical first response is to try and change our partner to match our expectations.

When we try to change our partner, we typically justify our behavior by convincing ourselves that it is for a good cause. After all, you are trying to strengthen the relationship by helping your partner become more of what you need them to be.

Just A Thought

Beware of molding your partner to match your fantasies. When your partner gets so far away from their true self that your fantasy is no longer a comfortable fit for them, don't forget how hard you worked to get them there.

What is the most effective way to begin addressing differences in your relationship?

Begin by examining yourself.

The only person you truly have control over is yourself. So, if you want to change a situation, the best place to start is with you. That doesn't mean you are the problem or that anyone is the problem. It simply means you are the best pathway for arriving at a solution you can live with.

Moving towards a better blend

Except in the instances of infidelity or abuse, a great alternative to "changing people" or viewing differences as deficits is to consider **"moving towards a better blend."**

What does that mean?

"Moving towards a better blend" means your partner doesn't "change." Instead, you begin to consider the fact that you have fallen in love with a wonderfully made individual that has attitudes, beliefs, and behaviors which differ from yours. When your endeavor to "change someone" is no longer your goal or expectation, you and your partner will begin discovering creative ways to find the balance.

NOTES

_____

_____

_____

_____

_____

_____

_____

_____

_____

_____

_____

_____

_____

_____

_____

_____

_____

_____

NOTES

NOTES

_____

_____

_____

_____

_____

_____

_____

_____

_____

_____

_____

_____

_____

_____

_____

_____

_____

_____

_____

Chapter 6

ROLES AND
RESPONSIBILITIES

JOURNEY NOTES

When you finally select your partner, understanding what that means takes time. In the beginning, you know you need to become more than you have been, but you're not exactly sure—more of what? The answer lies in knowing, sowing, and growing. This chapter addresses "knowing" by presenting valuable insights. The "sowing" and "growing" are up to you. Sowing involves evaluating which seeds of insight and information deserve to be planted and beginning to plant them in your own life. After that, the growth will come. Give your partner and yourself the gift of love, space, and time. If these elements are in place, discovery is inevitable.

Roles and Responsibilities

The smart couple realizes that "as early as possible" is the perfect time to discuss roles and responsibilities. When you address the issues of roles and responsibilities, you are simply asking, "How are we going to work together in this relationship?

What are roles?

An interesting insight often overlooked by couples is that roles reflect your expectations for your relationship. They are statements of how you view your function within the relationship. Discussing roles can lead to a wonderful journey of self-exploration.

INSTRUCTIONS: Below is a list of tasks. Complete the checklist by indicating who assumes/will assume "**primary**" responsibility for each task within your relationship. Place an "X" in the column labeled "Me" or the column labeled "My Partner." **Place an "X" in only one column for each task.**

Scale 6
Roles and Responsibilities Checklist

Me	My Partner	
____	____	Cook
____	____	Clean the house
____	____	Manage the money
____	____	Repair household items
____	____	Pay bills
____	____	Plan family vacations
____	____	Maintain the automobile(s)
____	____	Take out the trash
____	____	Shop for groceries
____	____	Plan family activities
____	____	Structure a retirement plan
____	____	Earn money
____	____	Help children with homework (or early learning for preschool ages)
____	____	Help children fulfill their dreams (sports, arts, etc.)
____	____	Have those difficult discussions with your children
____	____	Discipline the children

Next steps

Step #1 Review your Responsibility Checklist. Circle any "X" you would like to change, or that represents areas where you would like to do a better job working together as a couple.

Step #2 Exchange books with your partner. Review the responses in your partner's book and notice the areas where you and your partner differ.

Step #3 Return the book to your partner.

In one sentence, write what your responses to the Roles and Responsibilities Checklist tell you about how you view your role within the relationship.

Recommended Activity

Make this week a **"Week Without Blame."** In other words, make it a "Week of Responsibility."

NOTES

_____

_____

_____

_____

_____

_____

_____

_____

_____

_____

_____

_____

_____

_____

_____

_____

_____

_____

_____

NOTES

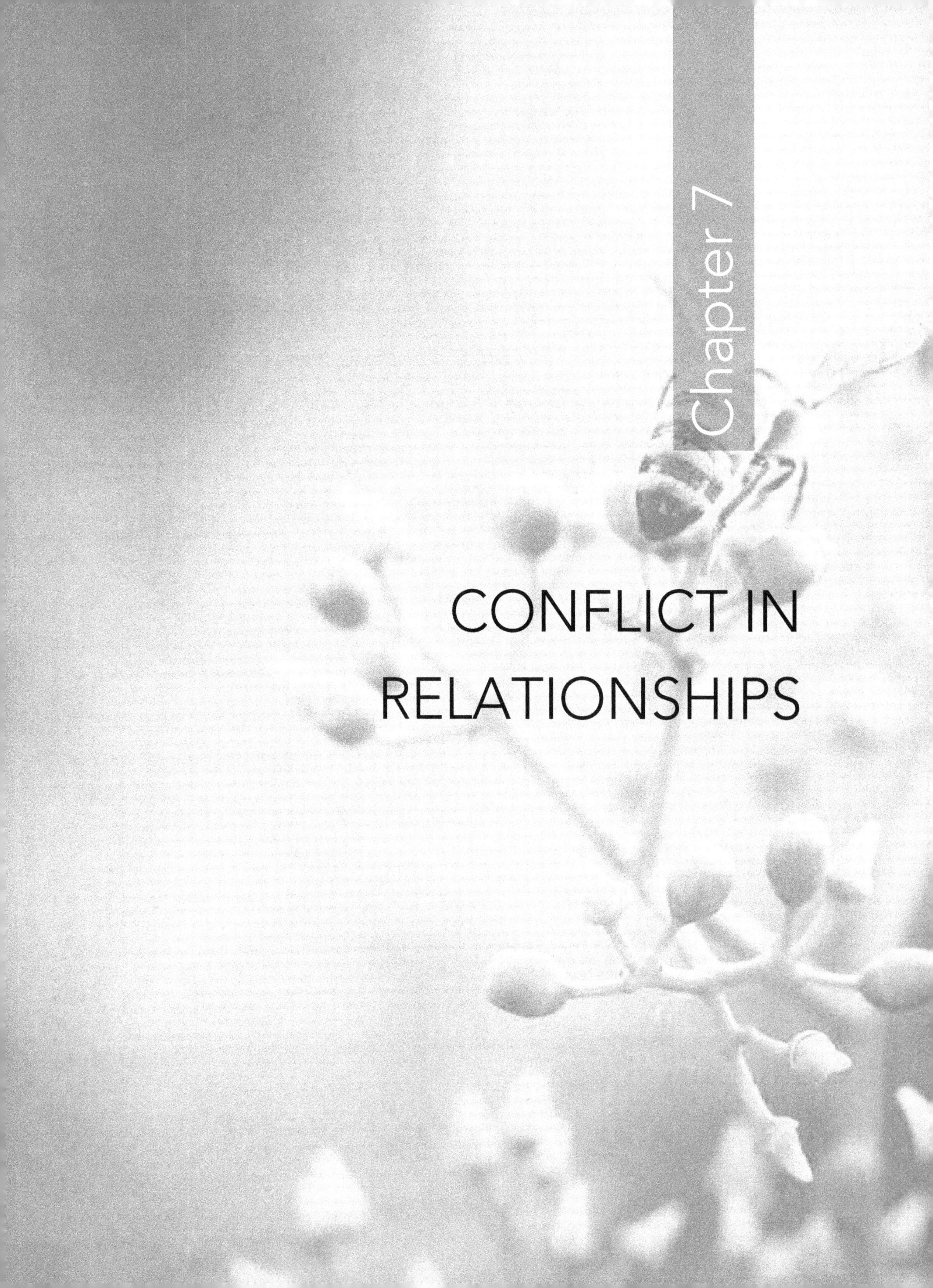

Chapter 7

CONFLICT IN RELATIONSHIPS

JOURNEY NOTES

It always seems so strange that two people would spend a lifetime trying to find each other, and once found, they start arguing about which direction the toilet paper should roll off the roller. Of course, there is an adjustment period in the relationship when you are learning about and adjusting to this new person in your life. During this time, periodic conflicts may be considered normal. But this period should not last ten years. The flip side is that some level of conflict is bound to happen. But even the inevitable can be a rare occasion rather than a common occurrence.

Conflict in Relationships

Why do we have conflicts?

All conflicts have the same origin. They begin with a disagreement when the thoughts and opinions of one person are not in agreement with the thoughts and opinions of another. In other words, they begin when what you perceive, need, expect, desire, or do is not in agreement with what your partner perceives, needs, expectations, desires, or does.

The probability that you and your partner will always agree in each of these five areas is highly unlikely. That means some form of conflict in your relationship will occur.

Let's take a closer look at the critical moments in relationships when the sweetness between the two of you is more likely to turn sour.

Key Moments When Conflicts Are Most Likely to Occur

Perspective	When your partner's perspective regarding life, society, and social order does not align with your perspective on life, society, and social order.
Needs	When your partner's ideas about what is necessary to be satisfied and fulfilled do not align with your ideas about what is needed to be satisfied and fulfilled.
Expectations	When what your partner expects to achieve in life does not align with what you expect to achieve.
Desires	When what your partner is wanting, wishing, and hoping for does not align with what you are wanting, wishing, and hoping for.
Behaviors	When your partner's actions and interactions do not align with your thoughts regarding how individuals should act and interact with one another.

How do you respond to conflict?

The question is not whether a conflict will occur. The question is, "How will you respond to conflict once it arrives?"

INSTRUCTIONS: Use the diagram below to identify your conflict response type.

Scale 7
Conflict Response Types

Where are you and your partner in this diagram?

1. My conflict response type is: _____

2. My partner's conflict response type is _____

INSTRUCTIONS: Show your partner your answer to Question #2 to see if they agree with your opinion.

Just A Thought	When your partner's perception of you differs from how you see yourself, it may be tempting to try convincing your partner of all the ways their perception of you is incorrect. However, it also may be a good idea to respectfully listen as they express their perception of you and work together to address whatever may be causing you to view yourself as misperceived.

Insights Regarding Your
Conflict Response Type

PROBLEM SOLVES   Those who problem solve provide the preferred response to conflict. It is the one style that pursues healing, meets the needs of both individuals, and works towards achieving the goals of the relationship.

COMPROMISES   Compromising always results in balancing between deciding which needs will be met and which needs will remain unmet. Often, a well-thought-out compromise represents the best you can do at the moment. However, it is important to remember that compromising is not the same as finding a solution. The real disadvantage of compromising is that frequently someone's principles and values will get lost along the way.

SURRENDERS   Surrendering is a self-sacrificing position. One person defers having their needs met to maintain the appearance of a harmonious relationship. Their behavior may appear honorable, but the potential for ongoing conflict will remain high because the stimulus for the conflict was never addressed.

DOMINATES   Dominating has a selfish goal. The person chooses to elevate their own needs and desires above anyone else. They are usually in pursuit of a victory rather than searching for mutual paths for healing and understanding. In your relationship, keep doing the math. Compare the value of winning an argument versus the value of living with a person who feels listened to and understood.

WITHDRAWS   Withdrawal occurs for two reasons: either as a method of avoiding confrontation, or if the conflict becomes intense, withdrawing is used to prevent escalation. Withdrawing to prevent escalation can be a wise choice if it is followed by efforts to problem solve. When your only response to conflict is to withdraw, the needs of the individuals and the goals of the relationship remain unaddressed.

We see that disagreements and poor communication are at the heart of conflicts. Therefore, we have dedicated the next chapter to identifying strategies for effectively preventing conflict. You will also learn how to manage conflict once it arrives.

Let's take a slight detour and use the last section of this chapter to address a more challenging topic that is important to mention.

When conflict becomes abuse

Let's have a serious talk about a difficult subject that does not deserve anonymity—abusive relationships. Whether you experience a toxic or abusive relationship, it is a distinction with very little difference. Both types of relationships involve a way of life that causes harm to others and must not be normalized or accepted. For those who may want to understand the difference between toxic vs. abusive relationships, below you will find a few signs of each.

Toxic vs. Abusive Relationships

A Few Signs of a Toxic Relationship	A Few Signs of an Abusive Relationship
• Controlling behavior	• Controlling behavior
• Overreacts to what is viewed as normal	• Calculated actions that manipulate others
• Conversations frequently become arguments	• Humiliates and demeans
• Their problems become your problems	• Extreme jealousy
• Everything becomes a competition	• Unrealistic expectations
• Blames others for their disappointments	• Isolates you from family, friends, and finances
• Views themselves as the victim	• Blames others
• More likely to criticize than support	• Ignores boundaries
• Easily irritated by unmet expectations	• Hypersensitive emotions
• Unforgiving and avenging	• Severe mood swings
• Toxic cycles and toxic behaviors that defy reason	• Violent physical, emotional, or sexual behaviors
• A lack of effective communication	• Premediated actions that harm others

Two hard truths to consider

1. If you are debating whether these signs constitute abuse, you are probably guilty of one or more.

2. If you are guilty of bringing these elements into your relationship and cannot acknowledge that it is abuse, you are not even close to your healing.

Whether you are the abuser or the abused, the behaviors listed above should not be ignored, normalized, or excused as a personality trait. Don't convince yourself that abusive and toxic behaviors will go away with time. They won't go away with time; they require your attention. Reach out to find programs, hotlines, and therapists in your area that can help.

NOTES

_____

_____

_____

_____

_____

_____

_____

_____

_____

_____

_____

_____

_____

_____

_____

_____

_____

_____

_____

_____

NOTES

_____

_____

_____

_____

_____

_____

_____

_____

_____

_____

_____

_____

_____

_____

_____

_____

_____

_____

_____

Chapter 8

THE POWER OF COMMUNICATION

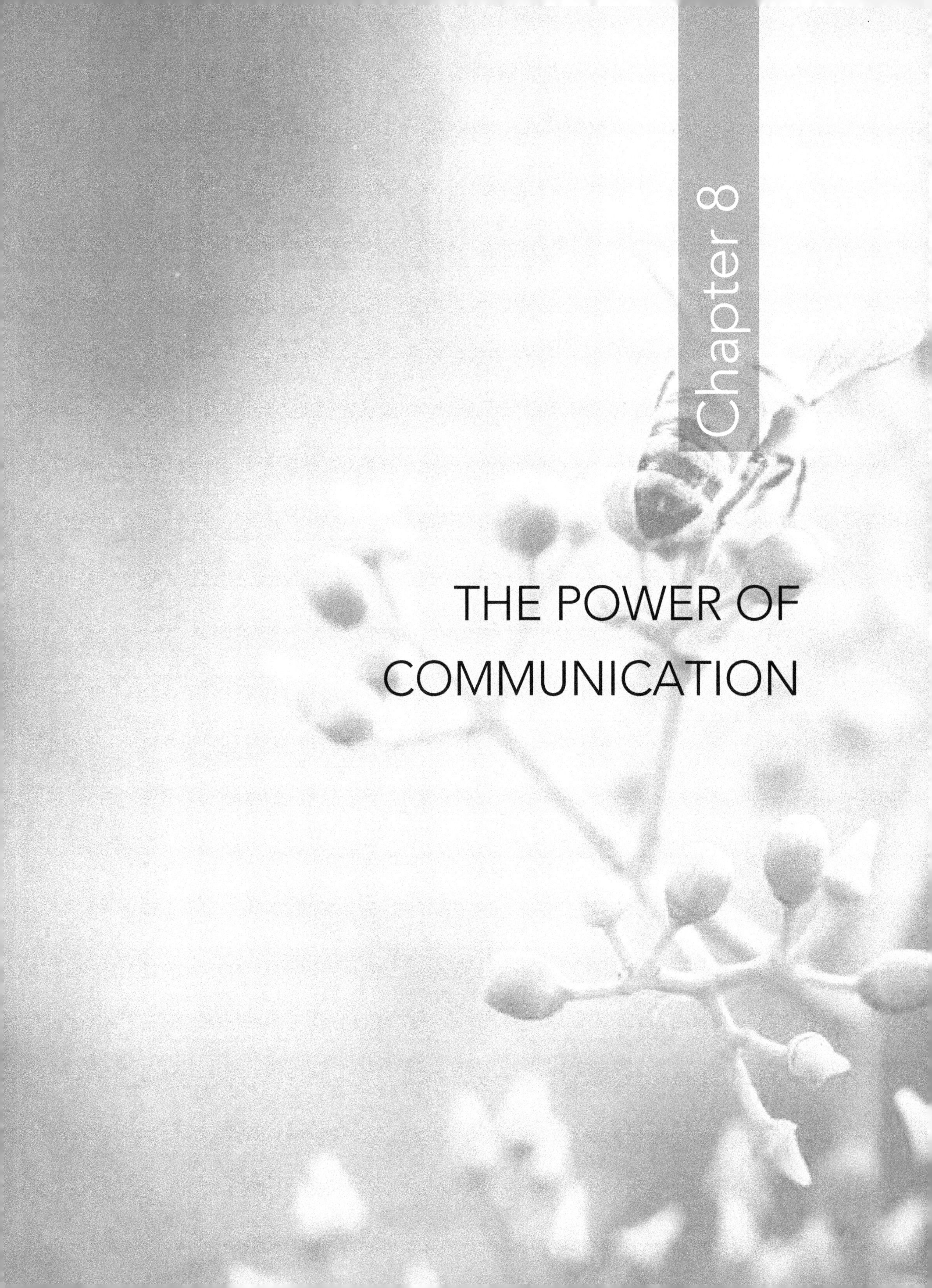

JOURNEY NOTES

"Communication." Something so essential to our relationships yet so fragile that it is always on the verge of breaking down. After all, you can put your words out there, but you can't control what anyone does with them once they leave your mouth. Once you speak and someone hears it, those words no longer belong to you. They are free to be interpreted or misinterpreted at the discretion of others. You know what you wanted to say. You're just hoping what you said accurately communicated what you intended for others to hear. Of course, what you hear is always filtered by your perceptions and expectations. Mastering this flawed and fragile process will be one of your most powerful tools for avoiding conflicts and misunderstandings.

.

The Power of Communication

Where do we stand?

1. I think my partner and I need to improve our communication in the following ways:

2. Identify your partner's verbal and non-verbal behaviors that have hindered effective communication in your relationship.

INSTRUCTIONS: Show your partner your answer to Question #2 to see if they agree with your opinion.

Just A
Thought

You may have the best intentions but if you and your partner are unable to effectively communicate, your relationship is destined for a progression of misunderstandings and conflict.

What is communication?

The Merriam-Webster dictionary defines "communication" as "a process by which information is exchanged between individuals through a common system of symbols, signs, or behavior." Notice that the word "talk" isn't anywhere in the definition. Talking is the easiest but not always the most effective means of communication.

What is your communication style?

INSTRUCTIONS: Follow the three-step process below to discover your communication style.

Step #1:   In the <u>left</u> column, place an "X" next to the statements that are true about <u>you</u>. Only complete the left column titled "Me" and make sure to continue to the next page. There are a total of 19 statements.

Step #2:   Now, exchange workbooks with your partner. Each person will complete the <u>center</u> column in their partner's workbook. The center column is titled "My Partner." Place an "X" next to each statement you think is true about <u>your</u> <u>partner</u>.

Step #3:   Exchange books to see where your partner has placed an "X." Circle the "X" if you disagree with their opinion. This step is intended to help couples see how their perceptions of each other's communication styles match or differ.

Scale 8
Discovering My Communication Style

Me		My Partner	
____	1 I hold my feelings in instead of expressing them.	____	1 My partner usually waits and gets revenge later.
____	2 I frequently sacrifice my wishes to please others.	____	2 Oftentimes my partner pretends they are joking while saying what they think or feel.
____	3 I am often silent about anything that would cause a disagreement.	____	3 My partner frequently outtalks me during disagreements.
____	4 I try to compromise so that we don't argue.	____	4 It is very important for my partner to win when we are arguing.
____	5 It is easier to give in than continue fighting.	____	5 When people try to talk over my partner, my partner keeps talking.

6	I am the one that usually starts the arguments.	6	When my partner and I argue, my partner usually wins.
7	My family and friends know that I will quickly lose my temper.	7	My partner makes sure to make their point during conversations.
8	I seldom say what I really think or feel.	8	My partner's friends and family consider my partner a good listener.
9	I raise my voice when we have disagreements.	9	My partner always speaks to me in a respectful way.
10	When we have disagreements, my partner's anger frightens me.	10	My partner seldom says what they really think or feel.
11	I usually wait and get revenge later.	11	My partner raises their voice when we have disagreements.
12	Oftentimes I pretend I'm joking while saying what I think or feel.	12	When we have disagreements, my partner's anger frightens me.
13	I make sure to make my point during conversations.	13	My partner's family and friends know they will quickly lose their temper.
14	When my partner and I argue, I usually win.	14	My partner is the one that usually starts the arguments.
15	When people try to talk over me, I just keep talking.	15	My partner holds their thoughts and feelings in instead of expressing them.
16	It is very important for me to win when we are arguing.	16	My partner tries to compromise so that we don't argue.
17	I frequently outtalk my partner during disagreements.	17	My partner is often silent about anything that would cause a disagreement.
18	My friends and family consider me a good listener.	18	My partner frequently sacrifices their wishes to please others.
19	I always speak to my partner in a respectful way.	19	My partner thinks it is easier to give in than continue fighting.

On the next page, you will discover what these "X's" reveal regarding the styles of communication you and your partner use in your relationship.

INSTRUCTIONS: Looking back at Scale 8, let's count your responses and answer the question, "What is your communication style?"

Let's Count "X"

How I View Myself: (Count the "X's" in the "Me" column only)

How many did you mark for statements 1 thru 5? _____ (Passive)

How many did you mark for statements 6 thru 10? _____ (Aggressive)

How many did you mark for statements 11 and 12? _____ (Passive-Aggressive)

How many did you mark for statements 13 thru 17? _____ (Assertive)

How many did you mark for statements 18 and 19? _____ (Considerate)

How My Partner Views Me: (Count the "X's" in the "My Partner" column only)

How many did your partner mark for statements 15 thru 19? _____ (Passive)

How many did your partner mark for statements 10 thru 14? _____ (Aggressive)

How many did your partner mark for statements 1 and 2? _____ (Passive-Aggressive)

How many did your partner mark for statements 3 thru 7? _____ (Assertive)

How many did your partner mark for statements 8 and 9? _____ (Considerate)

Find Your Highest Number and Discover Your Communication Style:

NOTE: Passive-aggressive individuals may have similar totals in more than one category.

My Results

Based on Scale 8, I think my communication style is _____.

Based on Scale 8, my partner says my communication style is _____.

INSTRUCTIONS: Look at the section above titled "My Results." Did you and your partner agree or disagree regarding your communication style? (Circle the answer that best describes your results.)

We
agree

We
disagree

Let's shift and focus on solutions! Below you will find eleven time-proven strategies that promise to make a significant difference in your relationship if implemented.

Strategies for Becoming a Better Communicator

Strategy 1:	Stay on topic. Don't drift away from the issue.
Strategy 2:	Take time to formulate your words even if you pause and return later.
Strategy 3:	Consider the consequences of what you say before you say it.
Strategy 4:	Don't use words like "always," "all the time," "everyone," or "nothing," which leads to exaggerated statements.
Strategy 5:	Instead of telling your partner what is wrong, tell them what you want.
Strategy 6:	Control your emotions.
Strategy 7:	Don't use words or voice tones with your partner that you would not want your partner to use with you.
Strategy 8:	Don't interrupt your partner when they are talking.
Strategy 9:	Don't spend time formulating your response/defense when you should be listening.
Strategy 10:	Don't include past failures in your argument.
Strategy 11:	Decide if the issue is worth an argument.

Recommended Activity

INSTRUCTIONS: Using the eleven strategies listed above, identify which ones you will use to improve your conflict style. *(Place the number of the strategy below.)*

Strategy #_____   Strategy #_____   Strategy #_____   Strategy #_____

Strategy #_____   Strategy #_____   Strategy #_____   Strategy #_____

Strategy #_____   Strategy #_____   Strategy #_____   Strategy #_____

NOTES

NOTES

_____

_____

_____

_____

_____

_____

_____

_____

_____

_____

_____

_____

_____

_____

_____

_____

_____

_____

_____

_____

NOTES

Chapter 9

SEX, INTIMACY, AND THE SIGNIFICANCE OF ROMANCE

JOURNEY NOTES

What a wonderful expression of our love. So, how did this gift we give each other become such a stumbling stone for so many couples? It often comes from two conditions: 1) burdening something wonderful with fears and inhibitions that have no rational context for lovemaking; and 2) not recognizing or incorporating the supporting cast members that are key to cultivating a fulfilling relationship. Those cast members include "intimacy" and "romance." Without intimacy and romance, sex simply has a singular physical purpose rather than allowing the intimate act also to represent your highest physical expression of love and affection.

Sex, Intimacy, and the Significance of Romance

What is intimacy?

Intimacy represents a closeness cultivated over time, resulting in an emotional attachment founded on reciprocal feelings of love, trust, acceptance, and attraction.

What types of verbal or non-verbal behaviors does your partner demonstrate that could potentially hinder intimacy in your relationship? Write your answers below.

Just A Thought

The verbal and/or non-verbal behaviors you have listed above represent habits, coping strategies, and other learned behaviors your partner has developed.

INSTRUCTIONS: Exchange books with your partner and complete the following steps.

Step #1: Read what your partner has written in the space above.

Step #2: In the space below, list the new habits you will commit to developing in addressing your verbal and/or non-verbal behaviors that are hindering intimacy in your relationship. When you have finished writing, return the book to your partner.

Let's not forget about romance

Romance represents a collection of expressions and behaviors that communicate a strong attraction or feelings of love.

INSTRUCTIONS: Place an "X" either in the column labeled "Me" or the column labeled "My Partner," depending upon whom you think is more likely to initiate the romantic behavior. **Place an "X" in only one column for each romantic behavior listed below.**

Scale 9
Who Is Bringing the Romance?

Within your relationship, who is more likely to…	Me	My Partner
Say, "I love you"		
Plan a romantic evening		
Light a candle		
Play/sing a romantic song/music		
Pass an endearing look		
Show affection		
Initiate sex		
Give an affectionate touch		
Give a kiss		
Give a hug		

INSTRUCTIONS: Look back at the two columns above and identify who assumes the greatest responsibility for the romance in your relationship. Place an "X" in one of the boxes below next to the answer you view as most accurate.

☐ Based on Scale 9, I have more responsibility.

☐ Based on Scale 9, my partner has more responsibility.

In what ways would you like to see your partner be more romantic? Write your answer below.

When you think of a romantic evening, what do you picture? Write your answer below.

Just A
Thought

It is important for couples to realize that sexual intercourse alone will not create an intimate relationship. It takes intimacy, romance, and sex working in unison.

NOTES

_____

_____

_____

_____

_____

_____

_____

_____

_____

_____

_____

_____

_____

_____

_____

_____

_____

_____

NOTES

NOTES

_____

_____

_____

_____

_____

_____

_____

_____

_____

_____

_____

_____

_____

_____

_____

_____

_____

_____

_____

_____

_____

Chapter 10

FINANCES AND GOAL SETTING

JOURNEY NOTES

Few things create more conflicts in relationships than money problems. Like it or not, we live in a society that operates based on two things: 1) money and 2) the promise of money (aka credit). If you disagree, you can turn on your television and be reminded every 60 seconds of this fact. Of course, the real tragedy is that most couples have more money than they realize but are unable to recognize it due to poor money management. Fortunately, all is not lost. There is hope and an answer for you.

.

Finances and Goal Setting

NOTE: This chapter is only intended as an introduction to financial planning and goal setting.

What is financial planning?

Financial planning is a way to regain control over your future.

What is the goal of financial planning?

The goal of financial planning is to move from managing by impulse to managing by intent. It is a gift you give to yourself and your relationship.

Which couples plan financially?

They are couples who desire to know where they are going and have a plan for how they intend to get there.

How do you recognize a couple that manages by intent?

1. They are not afraid to be accountable to one another.
2. Their financial goals and values are aligned.
3. They have the discipline to live within their means.
4. They view their relationship as being long-term.

How do you recognize a couple that manages by impulse?

They frequently buy things they don't need, using money they should be saving, trying to impress other people (many of whom they don't know), using possessions they often can't afford.

Which management style do you use?

☐ Management by impulse

☐ Management by intent

Which management style does your partner use?

☐ Management by impulse

☐ Management by intent

Let's dive deeper into examining your and your partner's relationship with money.

Net Worth Worksheet

ASSETS	YOU	YOUR PARTNER	JOINT
Cash on hand	_____	_____	_____
Checking accounts	_____	_____	_____
Savings accounts	_____	_____	_____
Money market accounts	_____	_____	_____
Certificates of deposit	_____	_____	_____
U.S. Treasury bills	_____	_____	_____
Cash value of life insurance	_____	_____	_____
Total	$_____	$_____	$_____
Investments			
Stocks	_____	_____	_____
Bonds	_____	_____	_____
Mutual fund investments	_____	_____	_____
Partnership interests	_____	_____	_____
Other investments	_____	_____	_____
Total	$_____	$_____	$_____
Retirement funds	_____	_____	_____
401(k) or 403(b) plan	_____	_____	_____
Annuities	_____	_____	_____
IRAs and Keogh accounts	_____	_____	_____
Other	_____	_____	_____
Total	$_____	$_____	$_____
Personal assets			
Principal residence	_____	_____	_____
Second residence	_____	_____	_____
Collectibles/art/antiques	_____	_____	_____
Automobiles	_____	_____	_____
Jewelry	_____	_____	_____
Other assets	_____	_____	_____
Total	$_____	$_____	$_____
Total assets	$_____	$_____	$_____

LIABILITIES	YOU	YOUR PARTNER	JOINT
Credit card balances	_____	_____	_____
Personal loans	_____	_____	_____
Student loans	_____	_____	_____
Automobile loans	_____	_____	_____
401 (k) loans	_____	_____	_____
Investment loans (real estate, etc.)	_____	_____	_____
Home mortgages	_____	_____	_____
Home equity loans	_____	_____	_____
Alimony/Child support	_____	_____	_____
Life insurance policy loans	_____	_____	_____
Projected income tax liability	_____	_____	_____
Other liabilities	_____	_____	_____
Total liabilities	$(_____)	$(_____)	$(_____)
Net worth	$_____	$_____	$_____

Cash Flow Worksheet

INCOME	MONTHLY	ANNUAL
Salary	_____	
Bonuses	_____	
Self-employment income	_____	
Dividends, interest, capital gains	_____	
Net rents and royalties	_____	
Social security	_____	
Pension distributions	_____	
Other income	_____	
Total cash available	$_____	$_____

EXPENSES		
Mortgage/rent	_____	
Utility payments	_____	
Home maintenance	_____	
Property taxes	_____	
Car payments	_____	
Car maintenance and repairs	_____	
Gas	_____	
Commuting fees/tolls	_____	
Credit card/loan payments	_____	
Life/health insurance	_____	
Disability insurance	_____	
Car insurance	_____	
Home/renters insurance	_____	
Liability insurance	_____	
Other insurance	_____	
Income taxes	_____	
Employment taxes	_____	
Clothing	_____	
Childcare	_____	
Food	_____	
Medical expenses	_____	
Education	_____	
Vacations	_____	
Entertainment	_____	
Child Support/Alimony	_____	
Charitable contributions	_____	
Gifts	_____	
Personal items	_____	
Savings/investments	_____	
Other payments	_____	
Total expenses		$(_____)
Net cash inflow/(outflow)		$_____

What we strive for is financial mindfulness. Goal setting is the pathway to get there!

Why does goal setting matter?

| There are two important reasons for goal setting | 1. To ensure you and your partner are headed in the same direction. |
| | 2. To agree on the destination so both of you will know when you arrive. |

Let's talk about barriers to goal setting

Eight factors serve as barriers, making goal setting difficult for some couples to achieve.

Reasons Some Couples Don't Set Goals

1. The goal seems beyond your reach
2. Fear of failure
3. A lack of interest in moving beyond your comfort zone
4. A belief that it will take too long to reach your goal
5. Procrastination
6. A lack of self-discipline
7. Deficit thinking
8. Not understanding the importance of goal setting

Here are a few helpful tips for those who find it challenging to set goals and equally as challenging to achieve them.

Keys to Effective Goal Setting and Goal Achievement

1. Set goals that are realistic for you to achieve
2. Set time limits for accomplishing your goals
3. Be specific in stating your goals
4. Stay positive
5. Avoid saying what you will not do
6. Use short-term goals to achieve your long-term plans
7. Outline a reasonable process for achieving your goals
8. Make goal attainment a priority

What goals would you like to work toward in your relationship?

Now, prioritize the goals listed above and compare them with your partner's responses to this question.

Goal setting as a couple requires "partnership." When you and your partner begin agreeing on where you are going, how you will get there, and when you intend to arrive, outsiders will become less influential in your relationship. You won't let friends and family walk into your life and get a vote on partnership decisions. The couple that can partner tends to have already recognized the value each brings to the other.

Be careful not to make the partnership just a business. Your partner needs you to value more than their contribution to the business and the bank account. They crave to be valued for all the parts of themselves they bring to the relationship.

NOTES

NOTES

_____

_____

_____

_____

_____

_____

_____

_____

_____

_____

_____

_____

_____

_____

_____

_____

_____

_____

_____

_____

NOTES

_____

_____

_____

_____

_____

_____

_____

_____

_____

_____

_____

_____

_____

_____

_____

_____

_____

_____

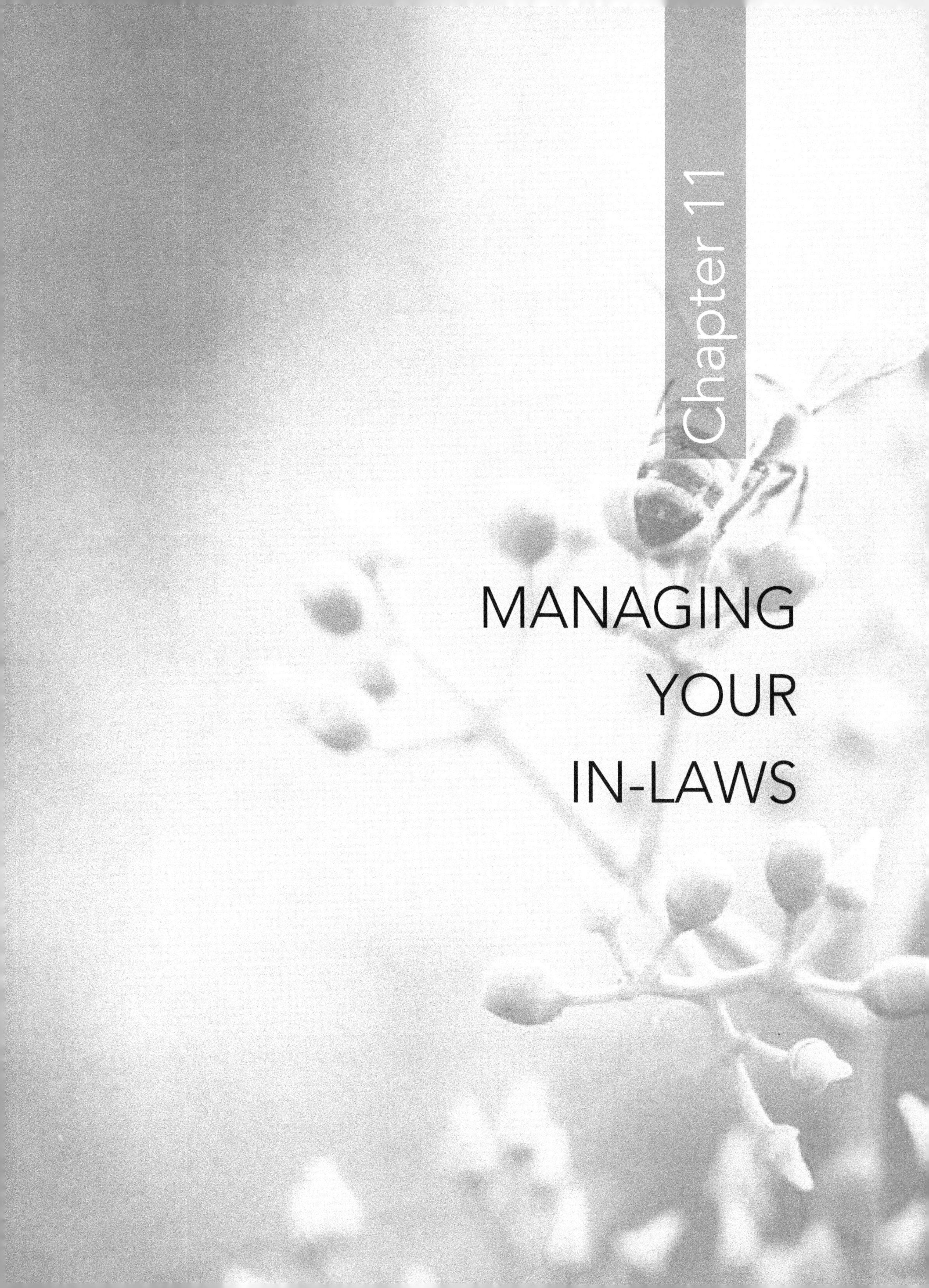

Chapter 11

MANAGING YOUR IN-LAWS

JOURNEY NOTES

In the lives of so many couples, in-laws are often in the position of being either a tremendous blessing or their worst nightmare, with little middle ground available between those extreme positions. Regardless of which one of these scenarios is your reality, it does not change the fact that these people are currently or are preparing to be part of your family. No need to fret. Within the following pages, help is on the way!

Managing Your In-Laws

Before we begin exploring your relationship with your in-laws or possibly future in-laws, let's take a moment to examine whether you have done your part to ensure a great beginning.

What do my in-laws expect from me?

As with marriages and long-term relationships, you have transitioned from being the person under the care of your parents or guardian to become the person they must now set free. How they adjust to this new phase of life is not only up to them, it is also up to you.

Their new boundaries, worries, comforts, and level of excitement are in many ways triggered by the outward evidence that you are effectively transitioning into the partner they are hoping you will be. Let's take a closer look at the various transitions they want to see.

In-Law Expectations for Couples

Emotionally - Transitioning your heart
Bringing your heart to your relationship. Whatever captures the heart captures the person. If your mother, father, siblings, or even extended family members have priority over your partner, achieving "oneness" will remain a distant goal.

Psychologically - Transitioning your mind
Placing your partner as a priority in your life as you both work toward a common mindset which is the key to living in harmony.

Physically - Transitioning your concept of "home."
Bringing evidence to your relationship that you fully embrace the responsibilities associated with the commitment. This is the first step in defining roles and responsibilities. Even if you live with in-laws, there should be clear boundaries, and your living arrangements should not compromise your partner's position of priority in your life.

Economically - Transitioning your finances.
Letting go of financial ties to family. Often these ties have the deepest roots, are the hardest to break, and can control and ultimately destroy a relationship. There is nothing wrong with receiving help. But couples also must learn to rely on one another. If you continue to rely on family for your financial needs, your relationship will remain a servant to the lender.

Spiritually - Transitioning your spiritual life
Transitioning your spiritual life means you are bringing your spiritual life into your relationship. There is no other transition that will have a more profound impact on your ability to achieve oneness than what you will experience through your spiritual growth together.

Question | Do you think your partner has fully transitioned **in all five areas** (emotionally, psychologically, physically, economically, and spiritually)?

(Circle your answer)

Yes   No

INSTRUCTIONS: If you answered "no," use the chart below to identify the areas where you and your partner still need to transition.

Scale 10
Transition Needs

(Place an "X" next to the area(s) where you or your partner need to experience a transition in your relationship.

	You	Your Partner
Emotionally		
Psychologically		
Physically		
Economically		
Spiritually		

A few of your thoughts

What do you enjoy most about your partner's family and why?

What do you see as potential points of conflict with your partner's family?

What do you think can be done to resolve these areas of conflict/potential conflict?

Read the passage below:

> Being in a relationship is like being handed a blank canvas with the freedom to create whatever picture you and your partner decide, using the colors of your choice. Now, tell us why would you hand your mother a paintbrush? Whenever you turn to your mother, father, or friends as a primary resource or decision-making body for your relationship, you have just handed them a paintbrush. What must it feel like for your partner to think they are designing something beautiful with you, only to look over and find out they are painting with their in-laws or possibly future in-laws? What statement have you just made to your partner about trust, commitment, and your belief in them to give you their very best?

What are your thoughts regarding the above passage?

Your reaction to the passage provides insight into your perspective/beliefs regarding setting "in-law boundaries." Differences between you and your partner in responding to this question may indicate that the two of you are operating from different premises regarding these important boundaries.

So, who is responsible for setting the boundaries?

Let's keep this simple. It is absolutely, unequivocally the responsibility of each partner to set boundaries for their parents, other family members, and friends.

Who should speak up?

It is important to be clear and direct regarding where you have set the boundaries for parents, family, and friends within your relationship. Some men sit and watch their partner combat his parents or siblings and label the issue "their problem." The same can be said for women who do not lend their voice when their parents conflict with their partner. Don't wait for your in-laws and friends to define reasonable boundaries for their level of participation in your relationship. They may never see that task as necessary.

NOTES

_____

_____

_____

_____

_____

_____

_____

_____

_____

_____

_____

_____

_____

_____

_____

_____

_____

_____

_____

NOTES

_____

_____

_____

_____

_____

_____

_____

_____

_____

_____

_____

_____

_____

_____

_____

_____

_____

_____

_____

Chapter 12

MY DISCOVERY PROFILE

An "At-A-Glance" look at your relationship

My Discovery Profile

INSTRUCTIONS: Add the total number of "X's" from each scale mentioned below. Place the total number of marks per scale in the specified area below.

Name: _____ Date: _____

Scales *(Leave shaded cells blank)*	Column 1 Me	Column 2 My Partner	Add Columns 1 + 2 Us As a Couple
Scale 1: Unhealthy Reasons to Commit (Pg. 14)			
Unhealthy reasons *(9 pts/person)*			
Scale 2: Threats to Oneness (Pg. 26)			
Individual *(7 pts/person)*			
Relationship *(5 pts/person)*			
External *(2 pts/person)*			
Scale 3: Qualities that Increase Oneness (Pg. 27)			
Qualities I do not show enough of in our relationship *(9 pts/person)*			
Scale 4: My Relationship Expectations (Partner's Point of View) (Pg. 34)			
Column 2 (I satisfy this expectation in my relationship) *(10 pts/person)*			
Column 3 (This should not be expected of me) *(10 pts/person)*			
Column 4 (This expectation is difficult for me to satisfy) *(10 pts/person)*			
Column 5 (This is an expectation I would like to achieve) *(10 pts.)*			
Scale 5: My Partner's Relationship Expectations (Pg. 35)			
Column 7 (Accurate) *(10 pts/person)*			
Column 8 (Inaccurate) *(10 pts/person)*			
Scale 6: Roles and Responsibilities Checklist (Pg. 52)			
Roles and Responsibilities *(16 pts/person)*			
Scale 7: Conflict Response Types (Pg.59)			
My conflict type (Pg 8) *(Write a response in the cell.)* (dominates, withdraws, surrenders, problem solves, compromises)			
My partner's conflict type *(Write a response in the cell.)* (dominates, withdraws, surrenders, problem solves, compromises)			
Scale 8: Discovering My Communication Style (Pg. 67)			
I think my communication style is *(Write a response in the cell)* (passive, aggressive, passive-aggressive, assertive, considerate)			
My partner says my communication style is *(Write a response in the cell)* (passive, aggressive, passive-aggressive, assertive, considerate)			
Scale 9: Who Is Bringing the Romance? (Pg. 77)			
Within the relationship, who is more likely to… *(10 pts/person)*			
Scale 10: Transition Needs (Pg, 95)			
Number of areas where transitioning is needed *(5 pts/person)*			

Interpreting My Profile

How to read the numbers

The actual number in each cell is less important than the difference between rows. Looking at the differences between rows will let you know where you need to focus more or less of your energy in working to build a strong relationship. The 1st and 2nd columns identify a primary origin for the various issues. The 3rd column recognizes that in a relationship, your issue becomes your partner's issue. It identifies where the collective energy of the relationship may need to focus as you view the "Couple" scores across the rows.

What do my results mean?

Scale #1:   Unhealthy Reasons to Commit

This scale addresses unhealthy reasons to commit to a relationship. It is designed to identify thoughts and perceptions that may not provide the best foundation for entering a relationship. "Couple" scores can range from 0 to 18. Any number above "0" is a reason for some level of attention. This does not condemn the relationship. Your score simply means that your relationship may have been based on a weak foundation.

Scale #2:   Threats to Oneness

This scale is designed to identify characteristics within you, within your relationship, and outside your relationship that could potentially hinder your movement towards oneness. These threats exist in many relationships and should not be a reason for great alarm. This scale simply signals you regarding areas to address in your relationship. As a couple, individual scores range from 0 to 14, relationship scores range from 0 to 10, and external scores range from 0 to 4. Use this scale to diagnose where your threats exist (individual, relationship, external or a combination).

Scale #3:   Qualities That Increase Oneness

This scale provides an opportunity to see imbalances in the relationship. This scale specifically addresses imbalances in the qualities couples need in order to grow and increase their sense of togetherness. In addition to seeing imbalances, you are able to return to page 27 and have a clear view of the target areas that need to be addressed.

Scale #4:   My Relationship Expectations

This scale identifies which of your marital expectations do not match your partner's expectations. Whatever your score, there is no reason for great alarm. However, it is definitely something you want to discuss together with your partner. Remember, expectations reveal your desires. If you are developing unrealistic expectations or mismatched expectations, you are setting yourself up to have unmet needs and setting up your partner to view themselves as unable to please you.

Interpreting My Profile (Cont'd)

Scale #5:   **My Partner's Relationship Expectations**

This scale identifies areas where you believe your partner has misunderstood your outlook towards relationships. Like Scale #4, whatever your score, there is no reason to panic but it is something you want to address. Remember, these expectations reveal your partner's desires. If you are misunderstanding their desires, you are setting up yourself to feel unable to please them. Also, you are setting up your partner to have unmet needs.

Scale #6:   **Roles and Responsibilities Checklist**

This scale identifies imbalances in who assumes responsibility for many of the tasks required to run a household. This scale is not weighted. Therefore, cooking has no greater value than paying bills or taking out the trash. Scores can range from 0 to 16 for either partner. As it is with most of the other scales in this workbook, the actual score is not as important as the difference in total scores (within the columns). Examining the columns reveals overall imbalances and identifies which partner bears most of the responsibility for maintaining the household.

Scale #7:   **Conflict Response Types**

This scale is straightforward. You are seeing how you respond during conflicts. Most important in this scale is the opportunity to identify any differences in how you view your response to conflict and how your partner views your response to conflicts. If you view yourself as a problem solver and your partner sees you as one who dominates, that is a discrepancy the two of you need to address.

Scale #8:   **Discovering My Communication Style**

If you have the courage to look, it is always helpful to have moments when we are able to see ourselves. This scale asks "what is my communication style?" This scale will not only tell you what style of communication you favor in your interactions, it also examines whether your partner sees your communication style the same way you do. Equally as important, when interpreting this scale, is to identify any differences between you and your partner.

Scale #9:   **Who Is Bringing the Romance?**

This scale identifies imbalances in who initiates romance in your relationship. Scores can range from 0 to 10 for either partner. As it is with most of the other scales in this workbook, the actual score is not as important as the difference in total scores (within the columns). Examining the columns reveals overall imbalances and identifies which partner bears most of the responsibility for initiating romance. Examining the rows of the scale will assist you in identifying specific romantic gestures you may be neglecting and need to incorporate into your repertoire of romantic expressions.

Interpreting My Profile (Cont'd)

Scale #10: Transition Needs

This scale addresses areas where you and your partner may need to experience a transition to fully manifest oneness in your relationship. "Couple" scores can range from 0 to 10. For this scale, a score of "1" is a large number. Why? Because addressing transition needs requires more than your "actions" to change. Transition needs are "areas" to submit. Any number above "0" is important to address if your goal is to experience the fullness your relationship deserves.

Scales #7 and #8 are not counted in the Discovery Profile.

Congratulations!

You have arrived at our culmination. You have made exciting discoveries, learned painful truths, found the courage to ask and answer new questions, and loved each other enough to listen. We hope it has truly been an amazing journey filled with life-changing discoveries.

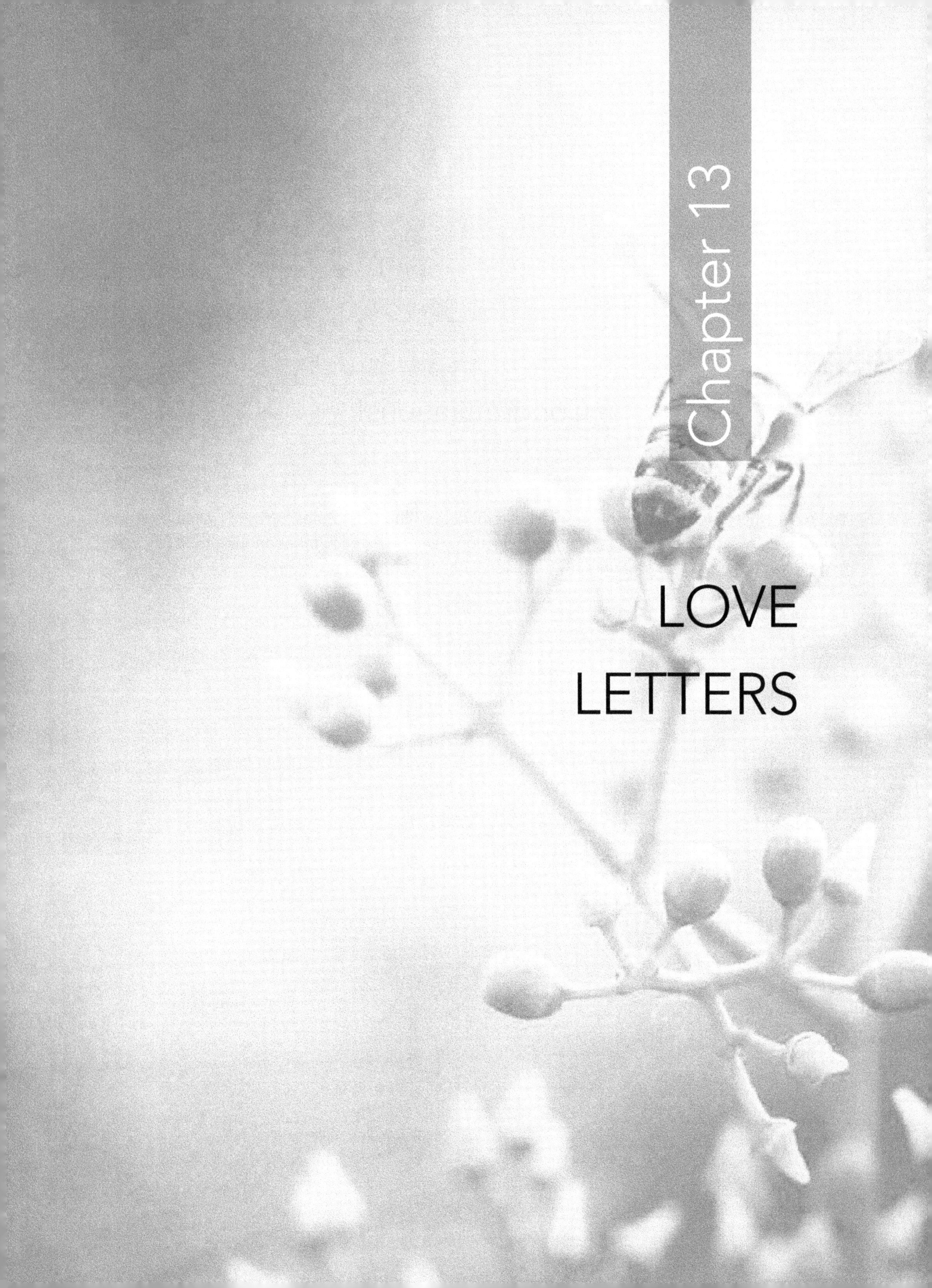

Chapter 13

LOVE LETTERS

JOURNEY NOTES

If you and your partner have arrived at this chapter you not only have a lot to celebrate, you have a lot to appreciate. As you have journeyed through this workbook as a couple, you have put your needs, confessions, and discoveries on paper. Today, you will put your heart on paper as each of you will use one of the templates on the following pages to write a love letter to your partner. One template is titled, "To My Partner (Template A)." The other template is titled "To My Partner (Template B)." Work separately and thoughtfully as you enter a time of heartfelt reflection and affirmation.

To My Partner (Template A)

Name one tangible gift and one intangible gift you would like to give your partner.

(A tangible gift is a gift you can see. Example: A house, flower, key, etc. An intangible gift is a gift you can only feel or experience. Example: Love, attention, commitment, etc.)

Tangible: _____.

Intangible: _____.

Use the space below to write a love letter to your partner explaining why you chose your gifts.

To My Partner (Template B)

Use the space below to write a love letter to your partner on the following topic:

"Why You Are the Greatest Gift of All"

If you have a story or a thought to share
we would love to hear from you!

You're the reason we do what we do!

contact@bemontent.com

A Product of

www.bemontent.com

www.ingramcontent.com/pod-product-compliance
Lightning Source LLC
Chambersburg PA
CBHW080252030426
42334CB00023BA/2791